Dedicat

I dedicate this book to my father, Orlando Flores. Thank you for your encouragement, support, and prayers at every stage of my life. I pray God will restore your vision until you are ready to join His heavenly reign.

Maria A Flores

grow in grace

This Book Belongs To:

_____

Your comfort delights my soul

Psalm 94:19

Large, Easy Flower Coloring Book

By: Maria A Flores

Touch the Heart, Reach the Soul LLC
Polk City, FL, USA

Large, Easy Flower Coloring Book

2024 Copyright by Touch the Heart, Reach the Soul LLC

ONLINE BOOKSTORE, APPAREL & GIFT ITEMS:
http://touchtheheartreachthesoul.store

Manuscript, design, illustrations, and book cover by Maria A Flores

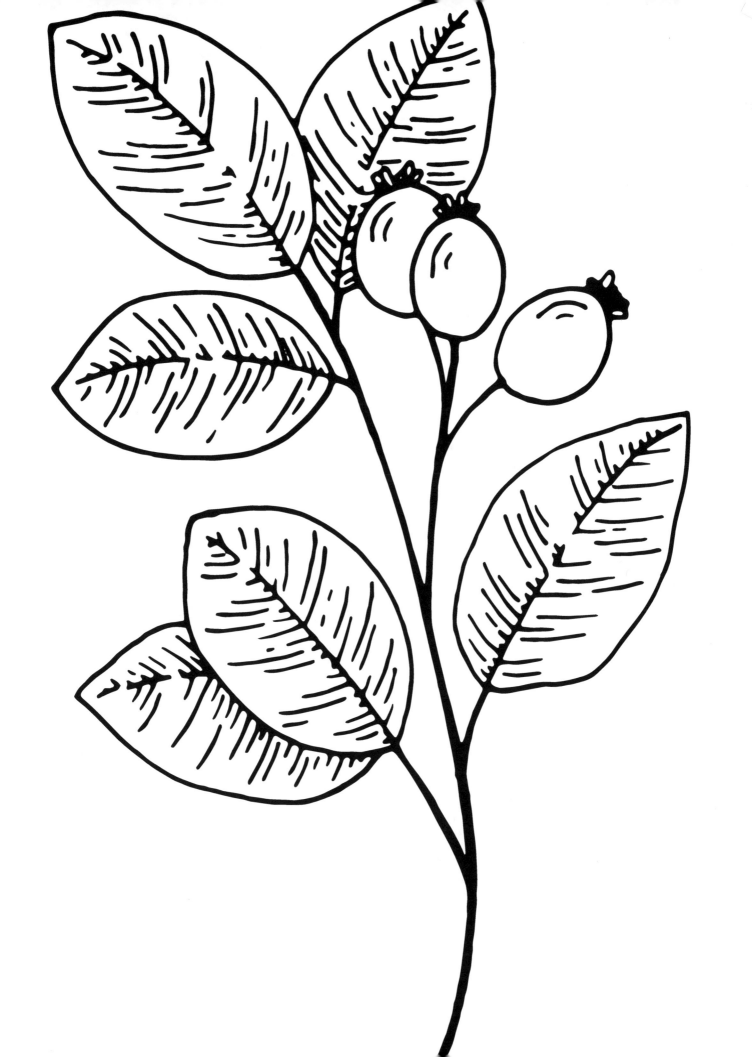

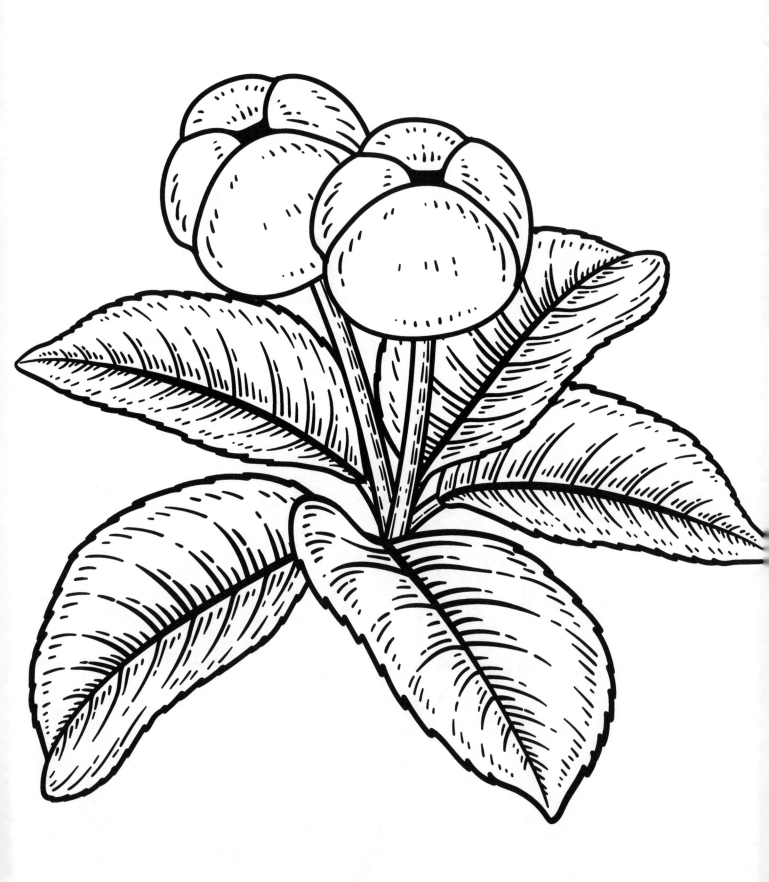

If you have enjoyed this book, please write a review on Amazon.

To see a full collection of faith based books, apparel & gift items from TOUCH THE HEART, REACH THE SOUL visit us at http://touchtheheartreachthesoul.store
Questions/Comments:
customerservice@touchtheheartreachthesoul.com

Made in the USA
Middletown, DE
03 September 2024

60017327R00068